GOD'S

FOOD FOR THOUGHT

Martin Kanizaj

CONTENTS

*I wish to thank my Lord and Saviour
Jesus Christ for persevering with me and
believing in me.*

*Also, my wife for her love and support
during the period of this publication.*

VI

INTRODUCTION

I have always had a fascination and love of words in my later adult life. Some three years ago some moral phrases started to enter into my mind. At first, I was a bit slow to understand what was happening. Some of them were lost to me. God by his Grace persevered with me and I connected the dots. This experience has enriched my life and given me greater understanding of my Saviour and Creator.

One thing that I am sure of is that I am a resident on the earth and only a citizen of heaven.

The best way to approach these phrases is to deconstruct them slowly, apply them to your life along with the Bible verses and to meditate on these with prayer to the Lord.

At times we all need to re-evaluate our lives. My wish and hope for all of you reading this publication is that it will bless you, bring any insights needed into your life and show you any changes needed to enrich your journey.

KNOWLEDGE

Wisdom is knowing who (God) butters your bread.

(Bible co-ordinate: Isaiah 41:10, 13)

****

God is victorious over every mess in your life.

(Bible co-ordinate: Joshua 1:9)

****

UNDERSTANDING

God doesn't require lip service. God requires life service.

(Bible co-ordinate: Isaiah 29:13&17)

****

To know and walk with God you need to walk beyond your own understanding.

(Bible co-ordinate: Proverbs 3:5-6)

****

Knowing the Lord brings you joy in your life instead of misery in your bones.

(Bible co-ordinates: Romans 15:13, Romans 12:12)

****

Don't get caught up in the world. Get caught up in God.

(Bible co-ordinate: Matthew 5:6)

****

We all need to abandon our mindsets and embrace God's mindset.

(Bible co-ordinates: Hebrews 3:15, Acts 5:29, Proverbs 3:5)

****

HELPFUL

Grace has no boundaries. Its power extends to the ends of the earth.

(Bible co-ordinate: 2 Corinthians 9:8)

****

AN INVITATION

The desert is full of sand and the sea is full of life. Jesus Christ is waiting for you at the edge of the seashore.

(Bible co-ordinates: Isaiah 43:19, Revelation 3:20)

****

TRUTH

A life lived without God is lonely.

(Bible co-ordinate: Psalm 25:16-18)

****

When you're a lost soul, God chips away at you, a piece at a time to become a masterpiece.

(Bible co-ordinates: Ephesians 2:10, Psalm 139:13-14, Luke 15:4-7)

****

You can't believe everything that you see and hear in the world. But you can believe everything that comes out of the mouth of God.

(Bible co-ordinate: Matthew 4:4)

****

Everything on the earth is perishable including all of mankind.

(Bible co-ordinates: 2 Peter 3:10-11, John 3:16)

****

AN INCENTIVE

There are two rewards on offer in the world. Only one is permanent and eternal.

(Bible co-ordinate: Ephesians 2:1-6)

****

A REALISATION

The scales of justice are always tipped in the Lord's favour.

(Bible co-ordinate: Psalm 33:5)

****

There is new life in the Jesus app. So, do you have the Jesus App?

(Bible co-ordinate: 2 Corinthians5:17)

****

We all need to realise that it was our sin that put Jesus Christ on the cross. So, confess your sin to God and be cleansed.

(Bible co-ordinate: Acts 2:23-24)

****

DETERMINATION

When setbacks come along prayer has to be your warrior.

(Bible co-ordinates: 1 Timothy 2:1, Ephesians 6:10-18

****

INSPIRATION

The bread of life feeds the weary and hungry.

(Bible co-ordinate: John 6:35)

****

POSITIVITY

The world is falling apart. You don't have to fall apart. Fix your eyes on Jesus.

(Bible co-ordinate: Hebrews 12:1-2)

****

Praying hands encourage a praising heart.

(Bible co-ordinates: Philippians 4:6, Psalm 63:4)

****

In our suffering and pain, God fine tunes us to his word and ways.

(Bible co-ordinate: John 3:16)

****

When coming to know God, he feeds us spiritual milk as an infant, like a mother who feeds her child.

(Bible co-ordinate: 1 Peter 2:2-3)

****

The world looks at life in dollars and cents. The Godly look at life with common sense.

(Bible co-ordinate: Matthew 6:24)

****

As infants of the world, we were short sighted. As children of God, we are long sighted.

(Bible co-ordinate: 2 Corinthians 5:7)

****

The world looks to bound you up in chains. The Lord looks to set you free from those chains.

(Bible co-ordinate: Romans 6:7-8)

****

An evil man only prospers for the moment, whereas a man of integrity is blessed forever.

(Bible co-ordinates: Titus 2:7, Proverbs 16:4-5)

****

There are only two good things that can be taken to the grave. They are salvation and faith in God.

(Bible co-ordinate: Hosea 13:14)

****

The Lord, Jesus Christ is the truth and life blood of all mankind.

(Bible co-ordinate: John 14:6)

****

The knowledge and love of God surpasses all boundaries.

(Bible co-ordinate: 1 Peter 1:2)

****

What you see is transparent, but what you don't see is pure and shiny far beyond all worldly boundaries.

(Bible co-ordinates: Psalm 12:6, Psalm 18:30)

****

You can't buy love, kindness and forgiveness. You can give it and receive it. God is the biggest giver and receiver

(Bible co-ordinates: 1 Corinthians 13:4, Daniel 9:9)

****

Don't streamline your life. Streamline your soul.

(Bible co-ordinate: Romans 8:11)

* * * * * * * * * * * *

The Lord is a bright ray of sunshine. Sit in his presence and let him invigorate you.

(Bible co-ordinate: Philippians 2:13)

* * * * * * * * * * * *

Let God strip you back to basics, layer by layer to properly honour and praise him.

(Bible co-ordinates: Psalm 100:4, Psalm 95:2-3, Psalm 69:30)

* * * * * * * * * * * *

Life without God is a wasteland. Life with God gives you faith, hope, love and a future, a path towards heaven.

(Bible co-ordinates: John 11:25-26, John 17:3)

* * * * * * * * * * * *

At times in your life God takes you by the hand and guides you.

(Bible co-ordinates: Proverbs 3:6, Psalm 25:4-5, Isaiah 30:21)

****

The world loves the dances of wolves. The Godly love the dances of souls.

(Bible co-ordinate: Romans 12:2)

****

The Lord's path is clear. The world's path is riddled with confusion.

(Bible co-ordinate: Psalm 16:11)

****

Every day we are going into battle against the world. So, we need to put on the armour of God.

(Bible co-ordinate: Ephesians 6:10-18)

****

When you are lost the Lord Jesus Christ comes searching for you, for he is the good shepherd. When he finds you, Jesus Christ gathers you around him to keep you safe and secure.

(Bible co-ordinate: Luke 15:4-7)

* * * * * * * * * * * *

Jesus Christ is the torch in the dark passages of your life. Follow him.

(Bible co-ordinate: Jeremiah 29:11)

* * * * * * * * * * * *

Is the Lord Jesus Christ your compass to the promised land?

(Bible co-ordinate: Proverbs 3:5-6)

* * * * * * * * * * * *

In God your life is a pre-planned road map. Which direction will you take?

(Bible co-ordinates: Proverbs 16:3, Proverbs 20:24)

* * * * * * * * * * * *

The Holy Spirit is your compass to the promised land.

(Bible co-ordinates: John 16:13, Job 33:4, Galatians 5:25)

****

Let God guide your every step and path.

(Bible co-ordinate: Proverbs 19:21)

****

QUESTIONS

You are born to breathe, smell and touch. So, do you breathe in the Holy Spirit? Are you intoxicated with the aroma of God's grace? Do you touch other souls with God's goodness?

(Bible co-ordinate: Philippians 2:3-4)

****

Do you thirst for the Lord?

Every second

Every minute

Every hour

Every month

Every year of everyday

(Bible co-ordinate: Mark 12:30)

****

A PROMISE

Without God, darkness blankets your eyes. Only the guiding light of Jesus Christ can save you.

(Bible co-ordinate: John 8:12)

****

CHOICES

You need to choose which master you wish to serve. The world or God.

(Bible co-ordinate: Matthew 6:24-26)

****

Temptation is your master if you yield to it.

(Bible co-ordinate: James 1:14-15)

****

In our weeds God shows us our needs.
(Bible co-ordinate: 1 John 1:9)

****

Everyone has a date with their destiny.
Everyone has to choose which destiny
they want to have a date with.

(Bible co-ordinate: 2 Corinthians 5:10)

****

A NEW PATH

Don't live with baggage. Give it to Jesus
Christ.

(Bible co-ordinate: Matthew 11:28-30)
(a new path)

****

SECURITY

Shake off the world and put on the Spirit of God.

(Bible co-ordinates: 1 John 5:4, Acts 2:38, 2 Corinthians 3:17)

****

ADVANCEMENT

Time waits for no man's plans, but only for God's purposes.

(Bible co-ordinate: Proverbs 16:9)

****

GRATITUDE

Give thanks to the Lord God each day for everything. For doing so, you become less selfish, less self-absorbed and his grace covers your life.

(Bible co-ordinate: Psalm 100:3-5)

****

The height and depth of God's love is only comparable to the colours of the rainbow.

(Bible co-ordinate: Ephesians 3:18)

****

FREEDOM

Everyone is in bondage, at some point, to something and or someone. Those who choose the Saviour are cleansed and released from bondage to the world.

(Bible co-ordinates: Romans 12:2, James 4:7)

****

Give your burdens to the Lord so that he can break you free of your chains.

(Bible co-ordinates: Matthew 11:28, Galatians 5:1)

****

CAUTION

Don't trip over your tongue. Instead introduce your tongue to a new dawn and bright future.

(Bible co-ordinates: Proverbs 21:23 & 12:14)

****

HUMILITY

At times, we all need to take our hand off of ourselves and put it on God. For we aren't the greatest thing ever, God is!

(Bible co-ordinates: Proverbs 16:18, Philippians 2:3, James 4:10)

****

Everyone can be famous and rich. Not everyone can be humble in God.

(Bible co-ordinate: Proverbs 11:28)

****

FAITH

It is better to deny the world than to deny the saviour.

(Bible co-ordinate: Matthew 10:33)
(faith)

****

JOY

The Lord can refresh your mind, heart and soul and spirit if you are willing.

(Bible co-ordinates: Matthew 11:28, Isaiah 40:31, Psalm 23:2)

****

Don't drag your lips on the ground. Lift them up to God.

(Bible co-ordinates: Psalm 34:1, Hebrews 13:15)

****

HOPE

The stainless-steel rod is hard and shiny. Whereas the eternal rod is flexible and forgiving.

(Bible co-ordinate: Ephesians 4:32)

****

You don't need a passport to get into heaven. You need grace.

(Bible co-ordinates: Romans 3:23-24, Ephesians 2:8-9)

****

Open the gates of your heart, mind and soul. Let the Lord in. For the pastures on the other side are green and fertile.

(Bible co-ordinate: Psalm 23)

****

At the end of the rainbow where there is a brand-new horizon, Jesus Christ is waiting to welcome you into God's Kingdom.

(Bible co-ordinate: John 14:1-3)

****

INSIGHTS

Man can see 10 feet away. God can see 10,000 feet away.

(Bible co-ordinate: Jeremiah 29:11)

****

The glass eyed can only see their own reflection and the golden eyed can see beyond their own reflection.

(Bible co-ordinate: 2 Corinthians 5:7)

****

God isn't in the business of satisfying souls. God is in the business of saving souls.

(Bible co-ordinate: Matthew 15:26)

****

Don't be self-indulgent. Be God indulgent.

(Bible co-ordinate: 1 John 2:15-17)

****

The mansion on earth crumbles and falls into disrepair whilst the mansion in heaven is everlasting.

(Bible co-ordinate: John 14:1-3)

****

Without God, life is an establishment, a construction zone that crumbles.

(Bible co-ordinate: John 15:5)

****

REASSURANCE

God's nature isn't to tickle our ego. God's nature is to tap into our conscience.

(Bible co-ordinate: Romans 6:1-4)

****

Breath God

Live God

Love God

   For

He loves you

(Bible co-ordinate: John 3:16)

          ****

The Lord believes in you even when you don't believe in yourself.

(Bible co-ordinate: Psalm 37:23-24)

          ****

PREVENTATIVE

You have car insurance, you have house insurance, you have life insurance. But have you taken out soul insurance.

(Bible co-ordinates: Matthew 10:28, John 14:6, 1 Peter 1:9)

****

A REFLECTION

The outside of a champagne glass is shiny and reflective, but the inside is full of cracks. So, it is with life.

(Bible co-ordinate: Romans 12:2)

****

CAUTION

Don't only feed your physical body, but also feed your soul.

(Bible co-ordinates: John 6:35, John 6:26-27)

****

WARNINGS

Greed has no friends and takes no prisoners.

(Bible co-ordinates: Luke 12:15 & Timothy 6: 6-10)

****

Righteousness smells like a fresh rose. Evil smells like the stench of death.

(Bible co-ordinate: James 4:7)

****

Don't look to prosper your life. Look to prosper your soul.

(Bible co-ordinate: Psalm 103:1)

****

Temptation is the corruption of the heart, mind and soul. It leads to spiritual death.

(Bible co-ordinates: 1 Corinthians 10:13, Matthew 26:41)

* * * * * * * * * * * *

Don't set your tongue upon the world. Set your tongue upon God.

(Bible co-ordinate: 1 Peter 3:10)

* * * * * * * * * * * *

Selfish desires and wickedness have no goodness in them and sin destroys the soul.

(Bible co-ordinate: Romans 6:23)

* * * * * * * * * * * *

Good works without faith lack everlasting power.

(Bible co-ordinate: James 2:26)

* * * * * * * * * * * *

If you hunger for the things of this world, then your soul will never be satisfied.

(Bible co-ordinate: Colossians 3:2-5)

****

As long as the human heart is rebellious, it wars against God.

(Bible co-ordinates: Deuteronomy 31:27, Psalm 107:11, Job 24:13)

****

If you don't have the love, innocence, trust and gentleness of a child, there is room for sin and evil to thrive.

(Bible co-ordinate: Matthew 18:2-5)

****

Without God life is an illusion. Don't fool yourself. The devil is waiting at your door to come in.

(Bible co-ordinate: 1 Peter 5:8)

****

If you don't walk in faith, then eventually you will walk in ruination.

(Bible co-ordinates: Proverbs 28:18, Matthew 7:13-14)

****

Atheism is a corrupt way of life. It takes you away from God.

(Bible co-ordinates: Psalm 14:1, Ephesians 4:18-19)

****

Independent thinking away from God leads to dangerous living.

(Bible co-ordinates: 1 Corinthians: 14:20, Luke 15:11-32)

****

God's enemy, the devil looks to deceive and destroy you from his bag of dirty tricks.

(Bible co-ordinate: 1 Peter 5:8)

****

Without God, your life is a barren wasteland.

(Bible co-ordinates: John 15:5, Psalm 127:2, Proverbs 3:5-6)

****

PRACTICAL

If you are dissatisfied with a little bit then you'll be dissatisfied with a lot.

(Bible co-ordinate: Philippians 4:11-13)

****

NEGATIVE

Works of the body destroy the soul.

(Bible co-ordinates: Matthew 16:26, Psalm 42:11, Matthew 22:37)

****

Being lost in your own world, you lose the purpose for your life.

(Bible co-ordinates: Jeremiah 29:11, Isaiah 53:64, Psalm 119:176)

****

If you have memories without God and his goodness, then they are empty memories.

(Bible co-ordinates: Ephesians 2:12-13, 1 Chronicles 16:12, 16:15)

****

Unforgiveness leads to dry bones which results in death.

(Bible co-ordinate: Matthew 18:23-35)

****

SADNESS

Do you not realise that abandoning Jesus Christ on the cross with your mockery of this gift of salvation to you and your insults, whilst he extends his love to you. You are dishonouring him with your sinful life. This leaves you empty and to eternal condemnation.

(Bible co-ordinates: Luke 23:28-49, John 3:16)

****

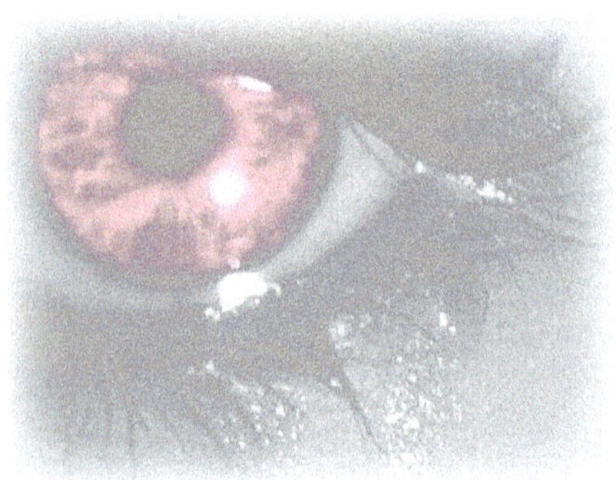

VICTORY

A snake can't defeat a man or a woman clothed in the armour of God.

(Bible co-ordinate: Ephesians 6:10-18)

****

PEACE

If you have turmoil in your life, the Holy Spirit can blow peace into your nostrils and calm your spirit.

(Bible co-ordinate: Romans 15:13)

****

COMFORT

The tears of a righteousness man heal the heart and soul.

(Bible co-ordinates: Psalm 126: 5, Ecclesiastes 3:4)

****